# The Spiralizer Cookbook.

Top 80+ Amazing Inspirational Recipes for Your Skinny Diet.

Your Free Gift

I wanted to show my appreciation that you support my work so I've put together a free gift for you.

LINK TO YOUR FREE GIFT

Just visit the link above to download it now.

I know you will love this gift.

Thanks!

Julia Nelson

Find other my books on Amazon clicking by link:

https://www.amazon.com/author/julianelson

Please leave feedback if you love them! It is very important for me

# Table of Contents

# Spiralizer

The Spiralizer is a device that will become one of your favorites for a vegetarian or rawfoodist kitchen, and for those who are on a diet or cook fruit and vegetable dishes for children. The Spiralizer turns vegetables and fruits into noodles.
Spiralized vegetables and fruits:
- save all the needed vitamins healthy for both kids and adults;
- make any dish decorative;
- are low-calorie and are perfect for those who want to get slimmer.

The Spiralizer will be your best assistant in cooking salads, main dishes, garnishes, desserts, fruit and vegetable chips.

# Spiralizer Breakfast Recipes

# Beet Omelet

Yield: Makes: 2 portions
Cooking Time: 12 minutes

## Ingredients

- 2 tablespoons olive oil, divided
- 2 small beets, peeled and spiralized with Blade C
- 4 large eggs
- Salt and freshly ground black pepper, to taste
- 1 small avocado, peeled, pitted and cubed
- 1 teaspoon chives, minced

## Directions

1. In a large skillet, heat 1 tablespoon of oil on medium heat. Add beet noodles and cook for about 6-7 minutes. Remove from heat and keep aside.
2. Meanwhile in a bowl, add eggs, salt, and black pepper and beat well.
3. In a large frying pan, heat remaining oil over medium heat. Add beaten eggs and with a wooden spoon, spread the eggs towards the edges of the pan. Cook for about 1-2 minutes. Place beets and avocado over eggs. Carefully, fold the omelet over the beet noodles and avocado and cook for about 2 minutes.
4. Cut the omelet into 2 portions and serve with the garnishing of chives.

# Potato & Egg Scramble

Yield: Makes: 2 portions
Cooking Time: 15 minutes

## Ingredients

- 1 tablespoon olive oil
- 2 small potatoes, peeled and spiralized with Blade C
- 5 eggs
- ½ cup avocado, peeled, pitted and cubed
- ½ cup feta cheese, crumbled
- 2 tablespoons fresh cilantro, chopped

## Directions

In a large skillet, heat oil over medium heat. Add potatoes and cook for about 8-10 minutes, tossing occasionally. Add eggs and avocado and cook for about 1-2 minutes, stirring continuously. Add feta and cook for about 1-2 minutes stirring continuously.

Garnish with cilantro and serve.

# Zucchini Frittata

Yield: Makes: 4 portions
Cooking Time: 25 minutes

## Ingredients

- 12 egg whites
- Salt and freshly ground black pepper, to taste
- 2 teaspoons olive oil
- 1 garlic clove, minced
- 3 cups fresh baby spinach, chopped
- 1 large zucchini, spiralized with Blade C
- 2-ounce feta cheese, crumbled

## Directions

Preheat the oven to 375 degrees F.

In a large bowl, add egg whites, salt, and pepper and beat well.

In an oven proof skillet, heat oil over medium heat. Add garlic and sauté for about 1 minute. Add spinach and cook for about 2-3 minutes. Transfer half of spinach into a bowl.

Place zucchini over spinach in the skillet evenly. Place remaining spinach over zucchini and top with egg white mixture evenly. Sprinkle with cheese evenly and slightly push into egg whites.

Bake for about 15-20 minutes or till top becomes golden brown.

# Baked Sweet Potato & Eggs

Yield: Makes: 4 portions
Cooking Time: 30 minutes

## Ingredients

- 1 tablespoon olive oil
- ¼ cup white onion, chopped
- 2 garlic cloves, minced
- 1 Serrano pepper, seeded and chopped finely
- ¼ teaspoon ground cumin
- ¼ teaspoon red pepper flakes, crushed
- 2 cups fresh tomatoes, chopped finely
- 1 large sweet potato, peeled and spiralized with Blade C
- Salt and freshly ground Black Pepper, to taste
- 4 eggs
- 2 tablespoons fresh basil leaves, chopped

## Directions

Preheat the oven to 375 degrees F.

In a large skillet, heat oil over medium heat. Add onion and sauté for about 3-4 minutes. Add garlic, Serrano pepper, cumin and red pepper flakes and sauté for about 1 minute. Add tomatoes and cook for about 2-3 minutes. Add sweet potato noodles, salt, and black pepper and cook for about 6-7 minutes.

Transfer the sweet potato mixture into 4 large ramekins evenly. Crack 1 egg over sweet potato mixture into each ramekin and sprinkle with salt and black pepper.

Bake for about 10-15 minutes or till desired doneness.

Garnish with basil and serve.

# Parsnip Waffles

Yield: Makes: 4 waffles
Cooking Time: 10 minutes

## Ingredients

- 1 tablespoon olive oil
- 1 garlic clove, minced
- 4 large parsnips, peeled and spiralized with Blade C
- Salt and freshly ground black pepper, to taste
- 1/3 cup scallions, chopped finely
- 2 large eggs, beaten

## Directions

Preheat the waffle iron and then grease it.

In a large skillet, heat oil over medium heat. Add garlic and sauté for about 1 minute. Add parsnip noodles, salt, and black pepper and cook for about 4-5 minutes.

Transfer the parsnip mixture into a large bowl and keep aside to cool slightly. Add scallions and eggs and stir to combine.

Place the mixture in a waffle iron and cook for about 5 minutes.

Spiralizer Salads and Side Dishes:

# Carrot & Apple Salad

Yield: Makes: 2 plates

## Ingredients

### For Salad

- 1 large carrot, peeled and spiralized with Blade C
- 1 large apple, spiralized with Blade C
- 1 cup fresh cranberries
- 2 cups fresh baby spinach
- ½ cup pecans, chopped

### For Dressing

- 1 garlic clove, minced
- 1 teaspoon sesame seeds
- 2 tablespoons apple cider vinegar
- 2 tablespoons extra-virgin olive oil
- 1 tablespoon honey
- 1 tablespoon soy sauce
- Salt and freshly ground black pepper, to taste

## Directions

In a large serving bowl, add all salad ingredients except pecans and mix.

In another bowl, add all dressing ingredients and beat till well combined. Pour dressing over salad and toss to coat well. Top with pecans and serve.

# Pear & Brussels Sprout Salad

Yield: Makes: 4 plates

<u>Ingredients</u>

<u>For Salad</u>

- 2 large pears, spiralized with Blade C
- 2 cups Brussels sprout, trimmed and sliced thinly
- 4 cups fresh kale, trimmed and chopped finely
- ½ cup almonds, chopped

<u>For Dressing</u>

- 1 tablespoon shallot, minced
- 3 tablespoons apple cider vinegar
- 3 tablespoons extra-virgin olive oil
- 1 tablespoon pure maple syrup
- 2 teaspoons Dijon mustard
- Salt and freshly ground black pepper, to taste

<u>Directions</u>

In a large serving bowl, add all salad ingredients except almonds and mix.
In another bowl, add all dressing ingredients and beat till well combined. Pour dressing over salad and toss to coat well.
Top with almonds and serve.

# Cucumber & Egg Salad

Yield: Makes: 2 plates

*Ingredients*

For Dressing

- 1 garlic clove, minced
- 2/3 cup plain Greek yogurt
- ½ tablespoon Dijon mustard
- Salt and freshly ground black pepper, to taste

For Salad

- 2 medium cucumbers, spiralized with Blade C
- 2 large hard-boiled eggs, peeled and chopped
- ½ cup celery, chopped
- 2 tablespoons walnuts, toasted and chopped

## Directions

In a bowl, add all dressing ingredients and beat till well combined.

In a large serving bowl, mix together cucumber, eggs, and celery.

Pour dressing over salad and toss to coat well.

Top with walnuts and serve.

# Beet & Quinoa Salad

Yield: Makes: 4 plates

*Ingredients*

- 2 large beets, trimmed, peeled and spiralized with Blade C
- 1 cup cooked quinoa
- 3 cups fresh baby spinach
- ¼ cup feta cheese, crumbled
- ¼ cup pecans, toasted
- 2 tablespoons apple cider vinegar
- Salt and freshly ground black pepper, to taste

## Directions

In a large bowl, add all ingredients and toss to coat well. Serve immediately.

# Zucchini & Beans Salad

Yield: Makes: 2 plates

*Ingredients*

- 2 medium zucchinis, spiralized
- 1 medium avocado, peeled, pitted and cubed
- ½ cup cooked white beans
- 1 tablespoon scallion, chopped
- 1 tablespoon fresh cilantro leaves, chopped
- 1 tablespoon extra-virgin olive oil
- 1 tablespoon fresh lime juice
- salt and freshly ground black pepper, to taste

## Directions

In a large serving bowl, add all ingredients and gently toss to coat well.

Serve immediately.

Ingredients:

- cooking spray
- 2 tbsp fresh snipped chives
- 2 beets, peeled
- 2 ounces chopped walnuts
- 1/4 tsp salt
- 2 ounces blue cheese, crumbled
- 1/8 tsp ground black pepper
- 1/4 cup olive oil
- 3 tbsp quince vinegar
- 1 (12 ounce) bag spring salad mix
- ground black pepper to taste

Directions

Preheat oven to 400 degrees F. Prepare a baking sheet with aluminum foil and grease with nonstick cooking spray. Using a Spiralizer, cut beets into spirals. Place beet spirals in a bowl; add 1/4 teaspoon salt and 1/8 teaspoon black pepper and mix. Spread out on the prepared baking sheet. Bake in a preheated oven, stirring halfway, for about 10 minutes. Let cool for 5-10 minutes.

Whisk olive oil, quince vinegar, salt, and pepper together in a small bowl to make dressing.

Place spring salad mix on a plate. Top with cooled beet spirals. Scatter blue cheese, chopped walnuts, and chives over the beets. Drizzle dressing on top.

# Spiralized Carrot and Radish Salad with Peach Vinaigrette

## Ingredients:

- 1 tbsp Meyer lemon-infused olive oil
- 1 tbsp shredded coconut
- 1 tsp peach-infused balsamic vinegar
- 1 large carrot
- 1 pinch garlic powder
- 1/3 daikon radish
- salt and ground black pepper to taste
- 1 tbsp slivered almonds
- 1 tbsp shredded coconut
- 1 tsp snipped fresh chives

## Directions

Whisk peach-infused vinegar, lemon-infused olive oil, garlic powder, salt, and pepper together in a bowl to make vinaigrette. Using a Spiralizer, cut carrot into ribbons. Combine with vinaigrette in the bowl. Let stand about 10 minutes. Cut radish into ribbons with a Spiralizer. Add to carrot mixture in the bowl. Garnish with almonds, coconut, and chives.

# Salad with Apple and Arugula

Ingredients:
- 1 apple
- pine nuts
- arugula
- crumbled goat cheese
- dried cranberries

## Directions

Mix dried cranberries and arugula in a bowl. Add a pinch of salt. Spiralize an apple, using a thick setting, and put it into the bowl. Mix well all the items.

Place pine nuts and crumbled goat cheese on top. Serve the salad with vinaigrette.

# Pesto Zucchini

## Ingredients:

- pesto sauce
- 1/3 cup of quinoa (cooked)
- 2 medium zucchinis
- pine nuts
- sundried tomatoes

## Directions

Boil the quinoa following the directions. Meanwhile, wash the zucchinis, peel and spiralize them.

Put zucchinis into a bowl. Add cooked and drained quinoa. Pour in the sundried tomatoes, a quarter cup of pesto mixture and garnish with the pine nuts.

# Zucchini Noodles with Lemon "Ricotta"

Ingredients:
- 2-3 large zucchini
- sea salt and freshly ground black pepper
- 1 cup cherry tomatoes, sliced in half
- olive oil
- raw cashew, for garnish

Lemon-macadamia ricotta:
- Half cup raw macadamia nuts
- Quarter cup raw sunflower seeds
- Quarter cup hemp seeds
- 1 garlic clove
- 2 tbsp fresh lemon juice
- half tsp zest
- half teaspoon sea salt
- one cup water
- 1 tbsp white wine vinegar
- Handful of fresh herbs: basil, mint, oregano or tarragon

Directions

Drain and rinse soaked (at least 4 hours) sunflower seeds and macadamia nuts. Add lemon juice and lemon zest, salt and pepper, hemp seeds, garlic, herbs, white wine vinegar and water to a high speed blender with macadamia nuts and sunflower seeds. Add a bit of olive oil.

Use a Spiralizer to cut the zucchini into noodles. Mix zucchini noodles with a few spoons of the ricotta, the tomatoes, a drizzle of olive oil and a few pinches of salt and pepper. Place an extra ricotta on the side.

## Asian Sesame Cucumber Salad

Ingredients:
- 2 English cucumbers, peeled
- 1 tsp white sugar
- 1 tsp salt
- 1 tbsp toasted sesame oil
- 2 tbsp garlic-seasoned rice wine vinegar
- 1 tbsp soy sauce
- 1/4 tsp toasted sesame seeds

Directions

Using a spiralizer, cut the cucumbers into noodles. Place cucumber noodles in a fine-mesh strainer set over a bowl. Sprinkle with 1/2 teaspoon salt and mix. Let cucumber stand about 30 minutes. Whisk rice vinegar, soy sauce, sesame oil, and sugar together in a bowl until sugar is dissolved. Add cucumber; toss gently until coated. Season with remaining 1/2 teaspoon salt; add sesame seeds.

# Cheese and Vegetable Noodle Medley

## Ingredients:

- 2 tbsp garlic-infused olive oil
- 1 cup shredded sharp cheddar cheese
- 1 Mexican squash
- 3 broccoli stems
- 1 yellow squash
- 1 pinch garlic salt, or to taste
- 2 Fresno chili peppers, sliced into rounds
- ground black pepper to taste

## Directions

Use a Spiralizer to cut Mexican squash, broccoli stems and yellow squash into noodles. Warm oil in a skillet over medium heat. Add Mexican squash, yellow squash, broccoli stems, garlic salt, and pepper. Cook, stirring constantly, for about 5 minutes. Add in cheddar cheese; cook and stir until melted (3-5 minutes). Remove to a serving plate; garnish with Fresno chili peppers.

# Soy, Garlic, and Chile Zoodles

## Ingredients:

- 1/2 pound turkey breast
- 2 zucchini, sliced
- 1 tbsp coconut oil
- 1 clove garlic, minced and crushed
- 1 red chili pepper, minced and crushed
- 3 tbsp soy sauce
- 1 1/2 cups chopped green beans
- 1 green bell pepper, chopped

## Directions

Using a Spiralizer, cut zucchini into spiral shapes. Warm coconut oil in a skillet over medium heat. Add in chili pepper and garlic; cook and stir for 3-5 minutes. Cut turkey into strips and add; cook, flipping once, until turkey is pale (4-5 minutes).

Mix green beans, bell pepper, and soy sauce into the skillet. Cook for 2-3 minutes.

Add in zucchini; cook, stirring constantly, for 2-3 minutes.

# Raw Beetroot Salad with Walnut Dressing & Goat's Cheese

<u>Ingredients:</u>
For the salad:

- 4-5 slices of goat's cheese
- 1 medium carrot
- 2 medium raw beets

For the dressing:

- Quarter cup extra-virgin olive oil
- Quarter cup walnuts
- Half tsp raw honey
- Quarter tsp sea salt
- 2 tbsp lemon juice
- Pinch of pepper
- 1 small garlic clove, finely diced or grated

<u>Directions</u>

Use a Spiralizer to turn beetroots and carrots into noodles.
Add dressing ingredients in a blender pestle and grind until fairly smooth.
Mix beetroot and carrot noodles with 2-3 tablespoons of the dressing (or more if you like) and place goat's cheese on top.

# Celeriac Pasta with Walnut and Apple Sauce

Ingredients:

For the apple sauce:

- 1 big apple, cored and cut into pieces
- 1 tsp honey
- 2 tbsp lemon juice
- half tsp raw mustard
- 3 tbsp olive oil
- black pepper

For the pasta:

- 3-4 tbsp lemon juice
- 1/2 celeriac
- 1 small green onion, sliced
- toppings: pepitas, sunflower seeds, sesame seeds and fresh thyme

Directions

First peel your celeriac and make your pasta using a Spiralizer.
Toss pasta in 3-4 tbsp of lemon juice and set aside. To make the sauce, put the ingredients in a blender and process until you get a smooth mix. Add pasta in the sauce and add toppings.

## Ingredients:

- 1 cup grape tomatoes, halved
- 2 seedless cucumbers
- 4 tbsp Sabra Classic Hummus
- 1/4 of a small red onion, thinly sliced
- 1/3 cup pitted kalamata olives, chopped
- 1/2 cup crumbled Feta cheese
- salt and black pepper, to taste

## Directions

Use the Spiralizer to make the cucumber noodles. Divide the cucumber noodles onto plates. Top with olives, tomatoes and red onion. In the center of the noodles, add a spoon of hummus. Add feta cheese over the noodles. Season with salt and black pepper.

# Zucchini "Caprese" Salad

## Ingredients:

- 4 cups halved cherry tomatoes
- 1/2 cup light balsamic vinaigrette
- 1/2 tsp salt
- 1/2 tsp pepper
- 4 medium zucchinis
- 3 garlic cloves
- 1/2 cup lightly packed basil, julienned
- 4 ounces fresh mozzarella

## Directions

In a large bowl, combine the halved cherry tomatoes, garlic, balsamic vinaigrette, salt and pepper. Use a Spiralizer to make zucchini noodles. Add the zucchini and mozzarella to the bowl. Toss to combine and set aside for 10 minutes for flavors to combine. Top with julienned basil.

# Mango Zucchini Salad with "Faux" Parmesan

## Ingredients:

- 3 medium zucchinis, trimmed

For the sauce

- 1 mango
- 1 tbsp blackstrap molasses
- 3 dates
- 1 tbsp chia seeds
- juice of half a lemon
- 4 tbsp water + 2 tbsp water

## Directions

For the chia seed pudding:
Place chia seeds and 4 tablespoons water in a bowl. Give a gentle stir and set aside for 10 minutes until chia seeds have plumped up and absorbed water to create a gel.

For the sauce:
Once the chia seed pudding is done, add all the ingredients for the sauce into a blender. Blend on high-speed until completely smooth. Use a Spiralizer to cut zucchini into noodles; pour dressing over.

# Cumin Cauliflower Cream Sauce with Carrot Noodles

Ingredients:

- 4 cups Spiralized carrots (skin peeled)
- 1 head broccoli (chop stems off)
- 1 head purple cauliflower
- 1 tsp cumin
- 1/4 cup unflavored non-dairy milk
- 1/8 cup coconut milk
- 1/8 cup nutritional yeast
- sea salt to taste

Directions

Boil 5 cups of water. Cut off stems and break apart cauliflower and place in uncovered pot.
Simmer until cauliflower is completely soft (10 minutes). Drain cauliflower and place in a blender with the cumin, coconut milk, nutritional yeast, salt, and almond milk, and then blend on high-speed until creamy and completely smooth.
Boil 6 cups water. Add Spiralized carrots to the water. Simmer for 3-4 minutes. Add broccoli. Continue to simmer for another 2 minutes. Drain carrots and broccoli.
Either warm sauce up in microwave or pour sauce as it is over carrots and broccoli.

## Ingredients:

- 5 cups Spiralized zucchini
- 2 cups cherry tomatoes, halved
- 1 can corn, drained
- 1 medium red pepper, diced
- 1 19oz can black beans, drained
- 2-3 tbsp lime juice
- 1 1/2 tablespoons chili powder
- 1/4 tsp cayenne
- 1 tsp cumin
- 1/4 tsp salt (or to taste)
- 1/2 tsp garlic salt
- pepper to taste
- 2-3 tbsp lime juice
- 1/4 cup cilantro leaves (for garnish)

## Directions

Place Spiralized zucchini noodles in a bowl. Using large tongs, coat zucchini noodles with spices (cumin, salt, pepper, chili powder, cayenne, garlic salt) until evenly distributed. Add in black beans and red pepper. Gently mix in cherry tomato halves and garnish with salt and pepper to taste. Stir lime juice in (if serving right away). Garnish with cilantro leaves.

# Zucchini Mint Springtime Pineapple Salad

Ingredients:
- 2 cups pineapple, diced into 1/4" chunks
- 4 cups Spiralized zucchini
- 1/2 cup sliced mint leaves
- juice of 1 lime
- 1 1/2 tbsp high quality olive oil
- 1/2 tsp sea salt

Directions

Gently mix pineapple, Spiralized zucchini, sliced mint leaves and olive oil in a large bowl with tongs. Before serving, sprinkle on lime juice and sea salt.

# Avocado Cream Sauce over Zucchini Noodles

## Ingredients:

- 2 avocadoes
- 3 zucchini
- 3 carrots
- 1/4 cup sunflower oil + 1 tsp
- 1 tbsp fresh cilantro
- 1 tsp cumin + 1/2 tsp cumin
- 1/4 tsp turmeric
- salt and pepper, to taste
- juice of 1 lemon

## Directions

For the noodles:
Using a Spiralizer, cut carrots and zucchinis into noodles. Sauté carrot for 1-2 minutes in a teaspoon of olive oil and 1/4 tsp cumin. Add zucchini and continue sauté for 5-6 minutes more until both veggies are soft to touch. While zucchini and carrots cook, create sauce.

Remove veggies from heat and drain in a colander for 5 minutes.

For the sauce:
In a high-speed blender, place avocados, cumin, turmeric, lemon juice, salt, pepper, sunflower oil, and cilantro. Puree until creamy.

Top noodles with the sauce.

# Soups

# Carrot Soup

Yield: Makes: 4 bowls
Cooking Time: 15 minutes

## Ingredients

- 2 teaspoons olive oil
- 1 small white onion, chopped
- 2 celery stalks, chopped
- 2 garlic cloves, minced
- Salt and freshly ground black pepper, to taste
- 6 cups vegetable broth
- 1 large carrot, peeled and spiralized with Blade C
- 8-ounce fresh button mushrooms, sliced thinly
- 3 scallions, chopped

## Directions

1. In a large pan, heat oil over medium heat. Add onion, celery, and garlic and sauté for about 4-5 minutes. Add broth and bring to a boil and cook for about 1-2 minutes. Add carrot and mushrooms and bring to a boil. Cook for about 4-5 minutes. Stir in scallion and cook for about 2 minutes.
2. Serve hot.

# Mixed Veggie Soup

Yield: Makes: 6 bowls
Cooking Time: 40 minutes

## Ingredients

- 5 tablespoons olive oil, divided
- 4-ounce bacon slices, cut into ¼-inch pieces
- 1 large red onion, sliced thinly
- 3 garlic cloves, minced
- 1 tablespoon fresh basil, chopped finely
- 1 tablespoon fresh thyme, chopped finely
- 1 bay leaf
- 12 cups chicken broth
- 1 large carrot, peeled, spiralized with Blade C
- 1 large parsnip, peeled and spiralized with Blade C
- 1 medium turnip, peeled and spiralized with Blade C
- 8-ounce Brussels sprouts, trimmed and sliced thinly
- Salt and freshly ground black pepper, to taste
- 2 teaspoons fresh lemon zest, grated finely

## Directions

Heat a large skillet over medium-high heat. Add bacon and cook for about 8-10 minutes or till crisp. Transfer the bacon to a paper towel-lined plate to drain and then crumble it.

Transfer 2 tablespoons of the bacon grease into a large pan on medium heat. Add onion and cook for about 8-10 minutes, stirring occasionally. Add garlic and sauté for about 1 minute. Add bacon, basil, thyme, bay leaf and broth and bring to a boil. Cook for about 15 minutes. Add veggie noodles, Brussels sprouts, salt and black pepper and cook for about 3-4 minutes.

Remove from heat and discard bay leaves.

Serve hot with the topping of lemon zest.

# Chicken & Zucchini Soup

Yield: Makes: 4 bowls
Cooking Time: 20 minutes

## Ingredients

- 1 tablespoon olive oil
- ½ cup onion, chopped
- 1 cup carrot, peeled and chopped
- 2 garlic cloves, minced
- 2 tablespoons fresh rosemary, chopped
- 4½ cups chicken broth
- 1¼ cups fresh spinach, torn
- 1¼ cups cooked chicken, shredded
- 1¼ cups zucchini, spiralized with Blade C
- Salt and freshly ground black pepper, to taste
- 2 tablespoons fresh lemon juice

## Directions

In a large soup pan, heat oil over medium heat. Add onion and carrots and sauté for about 8-9 minutes. Add garlic and rosemary and sauté for about 1 minute. Add broth and spinach and bring to a boil over high heat. Reduce the heat to medium-low and simmer for about 5 minutes. Add cooked chicken and zucchini and simmer for about 5 minutes.

Stir in salt, black pepper, and lemon juice and remove from heat.

Serve hot.

Yield: Makes: 2 bowls
Cooking Time: 25 minutes

<u>Ingredients</u>

- 2 tablespoons olive oil, divided
- 2 garlic cloves, minced
- 8-ounce New York strip steak, trimmed and cubed
- Salt and freshly ground black pepper, to taste
- 1 tablespoon fresh thyme, chopped
- ¼ teaspoon red pepper flakes, crushed
- 1 cup shiitake mushrooms, sliced
- 1 cup fresh kale, trimmed and torn
- 2½ cups chicken broth
- 1 tablespoon soy sauce
- 1 medium yellow squash, spiralized with Blade C
- ½ cup scallion, chopped

<u>Directions</u>

In a soup pan, heat 1 tablespoon of oil on medium heat. Add garlic and sauté for about 1 minute.

Add beef and sprinkle with salt and black pepper. Cook for about 8-10 minutes. Transfer the beef to a bowl.

In the same pan, heat remaining oil over medium heat. Add thyme and red pepper flakes and sauté for 1 minute.

Add mushrooms and kale and cook for about 2-3 minutes. Add broth and bring to a boil.

Reduce the heat to low. Stir in soy sauce and beef and simmer for about 5 minutes.

Add squash and simmer for about 5 minutes.

Stir in scallion, salt, and black pepper and remove from heat.

Serve hot.

# Pork & Sweet Potato Soup

Yield: Makes: 4 bowls
Cooking Time: 30 minutes

## Ingredients

- 1 tablespoon olive oil
- 1 teaspoon fresh ginger, minced
- 2 garlic cloves, minced
- ½ teaspoon dried thyme, crushed
- ½ teaspoon ground cumin
- ¼ teaspoon ground coriander
- ½ teaspoon red pepper flakes, crushed
- 1 pound lean ground pork
- Salt and freshly ground black pepper, to taste
- 4 cups chicken broth
- 1 medium sweet potato, peeled and spiralized with Blade C
- 4 cups fresh spinach, torn
- 1 cup scallion, chopped

## Directions

In a large pan, heat oil over medium heat.
Add ginger, garlic, thyme and spices and sauté for about 1 minute.
Add pork and sprinkle with salt and black pepper and cook for about 9-10 minutes, stirring and breaking with a spoon.
Add broth and bring to a boil.

# Ginger Zucchini Noodle Egg Drop Soup

Ingredients:

- 4 medium zucchini
- 8 cups vegetable broth, divided
- 2 tbsp extra virgin olive oil
- 2 cups, plus 1 tbsp water, divided
- 4 eggs, beaten
- 2 tbsp minced ginger
- 5 cups shiitake mushrooms, sliced
- 1/2 tsp red pepper flakes
- 5 tbsp soy sauce
- 2 cups thinly sliced scallions, divided
- 3 tbsp corn starch
- Salt and pepper to taste

Directions

Prepare the zucchini noodles with a Spiralizer.
In a large pot, heat the olive oil over medium-high heat. Add the minced ginger and cook, stirring, for 2 minutes. Add the shiitake mushrooms and a tablespoon of water; cook until the mushrooms begin to sweat. Add 7 cups of the vegetable broth, the remaining water, the red pepper flakes, tamari sauce, and one and a half cups of chopped scallions. Bring to a boil, stirring occasionally. Mix the remaining cup of vegetable broth with the corn starch and whisk until completely smooth. While stirring the soup, slowly pour in the beaten eggs in a thin stream. Continue stirring until all the egg is incorporated. Slowly pour the corn starch mixture into the soup and cook for about 4-5 minutes to thicken. Season with salt and pepper. Add the Spiralized zucchini noodles to the pot and cook, stirring, for about 2 minutes, or until the noodles are soft and flexible. Serve topped with the remaining scallions.

# Spicy Chickpea & Sweet Potato Noodle Soup

Ingredients:
- 1 tbsp coconut oil or ghee
- 1/2 tsp ground cinnamon
- 2 tsp ground turmeric
- 1 tsp hot smoked paprika
- 2 tsp ground ginger
- 1 tsp caraway seeds
- 1/2 tsp freshly grated nutmeg
- 1 pinch saffron (about 40 threads) soaked in.
- 1 tsp fine grain sea salt
- 2 tbsp hot water
- 3 medium onions
- 1 cup dried lentils, soaked overnight if possible
- 14 oz / 400ml canned whole tomatoes
- 6oz / 170g tomato paste (1 small can)
- 1 1/2 cup dried chickpeas OR 3 cups / 500g cooked chickpeas (about 2 cans)
- 1/2 cup / 20g flat-leaf parsley, leaves and tender stems only, plus more for garnish
- 1 medium sweet potato
- 3 slices lemon
- 5 cups water
- 1/2 cup / 20g cilantro, leaves and tender stems only, plus more for garnish
- lemon wedges for serving
- sea salt and freshly ground pepper, to taste

Directions

If you are going to use dried chickpeas, soak them in pure water overnight with apple cider vinegar or lemon juice. The next morning, drain and rinse.

Place in a large stockpot, cover with fresh water, bring to a boil and simmer about 45 minutes. About 30 minutes into cooking, add a tablespoon of salt. Drain and rinse.

Place saffron threads in a small cup with 2 tablespoons of recently-boiled water. Let steep for 10-15 minutes.

Peel and dice onions. Heat coconut oil in a large stockpot over medium-high heat. Add the turmeric, ginger, caraway, paprika, cinnamon, and nutmeg. Stir to blend, and cook for 1-2 minutes. Lower the heat to medium, add onions and salt, stir to coat.

Cook about 10 minutes (add a little water to the pot if it becomes dry). Add the steeped saffron liquid, the canned tomatoes, tomato paste, chickpeas, lentils, lemon slices and water. Bring to a boil; reduce to simmer and cook covered about 15-25 minutes depending on whether or not you soaked them.

While the soup is cooking, make the sweet potato noodles. Peel the sweet potato. Cut the potato with a Spiralizer. Wash the herbs well, spin dry and roughly chop, removing any tough stems.

Add the sweet potato noodles and herbs to the pot, stir to incorporate and let simmer for 5 minutes. Season to taste. Ladle out desired amount of hot soup into bowls.

Serve with a wedge of lemon.

## Ingredients:

- 3 medium zucchinis
- 1/2 heaping cup diced red onion
- 2 celery ribs, diced
- 1 small pinch of red pepper flakes
- 1 large carrot, diced
- 2 garlic cloves, minced
- 1 tsp dried thyme
- 1 tsp dried oregano
- 6 cups chicken broth, low-sodium
- 4 chicken thighs, bone-in, about 1.75 pounds
- 2 bay leaves
- 2 cups water

## Directions

Place a large soup pot over medium heat and add in the onions, celery, carrots, garlic and red pepper flakes. Cook for 3-5 minutes.

Add in the thyme and oregano and cook for another 1 minute, stirring frequently.

Place in the chicken thighs and bay leaf and pour in the chicken broth and water. Cover and let come to a boil. Once boiling, lower to a steady simmer and cook for 30 minutes.

Then remove the chicken and peel off the skin and discard. Then, shred the chicken off the bone and set aside, with any juices. Place the bones back into the soup pot and simmer for 10 more minutes, uncovered.

While the bones simmer, slice the zucchinis halfway lengthwise. Then, using a Spiralizer, cut them into noodles. Set aside. Remove the bones and bay leaves and discard.

Add the reserved shredded chicken back to the pot along with the zucchini noodles. Cook for 5 minutes.
Serve warm.

# Main Dishes

# Veggie Stew

Yield: Makes: 2 bowls
Cooking Time: 21 minutes

## Ingredients

- 1 tablespoon olive oil
- 1 small onion, minced
- 3 garlic cloves, minced
- 4 cups vegetable broth
- 1½ cups canned chickpeas, rinsed and drained
- 1 teaspoon dried rosemary, crushed
- 1 teaspoon marjoram, crushed
- ½ teaspoon smoked paprika
- ½ teaspoon ground turmeric
- 1 large carrot, peeled and spiralized with Blade C
- 1 medium celeriac, peeled and spiralized with Blade C
- 1 cup fresh spinach, torn
- ¼ cup nutritional yeast
- Salt and freshly ground black pepper, to taste

## Directions

In a large pan, heat oil over medium heat. Add onion, garlic, and red pepper flakes and sauté for about 4-5 minutes. Add garlic and sauté for about 1 minute. Add the broth, chickpeas, herbs and spices and bring to a boil over high heat. Stir in carrot and celeriac noodles.
Reduce the heat to medium-low and simmer, covered for about 10 minutes. Stir in spinach and simmer for about 5 minutes. Stir in the nutritional yeast, salt, and black pepper and remove from the heat. Serve hot.

# Sweet Potato with Meatballs Curry

Yield: Makes: 4 bowls
Cooking Time: 30 minutes

<u>Ingredients</u>

For Meatballs

- 1 pound lean ground beef
- 1 tablespoon garlic, minced
- 1 tablespoon fresh ginger, minced
- ¼ cup yellow onion, chopped finely
- 1 cup brown mushrooms, chopped finely
- 1 jalapeño pepper, minced
- 1 teaspoon Sriracha
- ½ teaspoon fish sauce
- Salt and freshly ground black pepper, to taste
- 1 large egg
- 1 tablespoon cornstarch

For Curry Sauce
- 1 (13½-ounce) can coconut milk
- 2 tablespoons red curry paste
- 2 teaspoons honey
- ½ teaspoon fish sauce

For Sweet Potatoes
- 1 tablespoon olive oil
- 2 large sweet potatoes, peeled and spiralized with Blade C
- Salt and freshly ground black pepper, to taste

<u>Directions</u>

Preheat the oven to 400 degrees F. Line a large baking sheet with a greased piece of foil.

For meatballs in a large bowl, add all ingredients and mix till well combined. Make small sized balls from the mixture.

Arrange the meatballs on prepared baking sheet in a single layer. Bake for about 13 minutes. Flip and bake for about 2-3 minutes. Remove from oven and keep aside.

For curry sauce in a large pan, add coconut milk on medium-high heat and bring to a boil. Add the red curry paste and beat till well combined. Stir in honey and fish sauce. Carefully, add the meatballs. Reduce the heat to medium-low and simmer for about 10 minutes.

Meanwhile in a large skillet, heat oil over medium-high heat. Add sweet potatoes and cook for about 6-8 minutes. Season with salt and pepper and remove from heat.

Divide sweet potato noodles into serving bowls and top with meatballs and curry sauce.

Serve hot.

Yield: Makes: 4 portions
Cooking Time: 45 minutes

Ingredients

- 4-6 medium yellow squash, spiralized with Blade C
- 3 tablespoons olive oil, divided
- Salt and freshly ground black pepper, to taste
- 1 pound skinless, boneless chicken breasts, cut into thin strips
- 1 white onion, chopped
- 3-4 garlic cloves, minced
- ¾ pound grape tomatoes, halved
- 1¼ cups chicken broth
- ½ cup fresh baby spinach
- 1 tablespoon fresh oregano, chopped
- 1 tablespoon fresh thyme, chopped

Directions

Preheat the oven to 400 degrees F. Grease a large baking sheet.
Place squash noodles on prepared baking sheet. Drizzle with 1
tablespoon of oil and sprinkle with salt and black pepper. Bake for
about 25 minutes, tossing once after 10 minutes. Remove from oven
and keep aside.

In a large skillet, heat 1 tablespoon of oil on medium heat. Add chicken
and sprinkle with salt and black pepper and cook for about 8-10
minutes or till golden brown from all sides. Transfer the chicken to a
plate.

In the same skillet, heat remaining oil over medium heat. Add onion
and sauté for about 3-4 minutes. Add garlic and sauté for about 1
minute. Add tomatoes and broth and cook for about 2-3 minutes. Add

chicken, squash noodles, spinach and herbs and cook for about 2 minutes.

Serve hot.

# Turnip with Lamb Chops

Yield: Makes: 2 portions
Cooking Time: 10 minutes

## Ingredients

### For Lamb Marinade
- 1 garlic clove, minced
- 1 teaspoon fresh rosemary, minced
- ½ tablespoon fresh lemon juice
- ½ tablespoon olive oil
- Salt and freshly ground black pepper, to taste
- 2 lamb shoulder chops, trimmed

### For Turnip
- 1 tablespoon olive oil
- 2 large turnips, trimmed, peeled and spiralized with Blade C
- Salt and freshly ground black pepper, to taste

## Directions

For marinade in a bowl, mix together all ingredients except lamb chops. Add lamb chops and coat with marinade mixture generously. Keep aside in the room temperature for about 15-20 minutes.

Preheat the broiler of oven. Arrange an oven rack 4-5-inches from heating element. Line a broiler pan with a piece of foil.

Remove the chops from the bowl and shake off excess marinade. Arrange the chops on the prepared broiler pan. Broil for about 5 minutes per side.

Meanwhile in a skillet, heat oil over medium heat. Add onion and sauté for about 4-5 minutes. Add turnip, salt, and black pepper and cook for about 3-4 minutes.

Transfer the turnip mixture in serving plate and top with lamb chops. Serve hot.

# Zucchini & Salmon Casserole

Yield: Makes: 4 portions
Cooking Time: 1 hour 10 minutes

## Ingredients

- 3 tablespoons olive oil, divided
- 1 small onion, chopped
- 1 celery stalk, chopped
- 3 garlic cloves, minced
- Salt and freshly ground black pepper, to taste
- 2 medium zucchinis, spiralized with Blade C
- 1¼ cups cooked salmon, chopped very finely
- 1 tablespoon arrowroot powder
- 1½ cups unsweetened almond milk

## Directions

Preheat the oven to 350 degrees F. Lightly, grease a casserole dish.

In a skillet, heat 1 tablespoon of oil on medium heat. Add onion and celery and sauté for about 3-4 minutes. Add garlic and sauté for about 1 minute. Stir in zucchini, salmon, salt and black pepper. Transfer the zucchini mixture to a casserole dish.

In another pan, heat oil over medium-low heat. Slowly, add arrowroot powder, beating continuously for about 1 minute. Slowly, add almond milk, beating continuously and cook for about 2-3 minutes or till thick. Pour sauce over zucchini mixture evenly.

Bake for about 45-60 minutes.

Ingredients:

- 300 g raw king prawns
- 2 large green zucchinis
- dollop of coconut oil
- 1/4 cup of grated parmesan
- One and half cup chopped tinned tomatoes
- 3 tbsp olive oil
- 1 brown onion, diced
- 1/2 red sweet bell pepper, diced
- 2/3 tsp salt
- 2/3 tsp chili pepper
- freshly chopped parsley
- 3 cloves garlic, diced

Directions

Use a Spiralizer to cut zucchini into noodles.
In a large frying pan, heat a dollop of coconut oil over high heat. Add the prawns and pan fry for 2 minutes, stirring a few times. Remove to a bowl. Turn the heat to medium and add the olive oil to the pan.
Add the diced onion and peppers, and fry for about 3 minutes, until lightly browned. Then add the salt, chili and garlic, and stir through. Pour in the tomatoes and mix well. Cook for a couple of minutes over medium heat, stirring a few times.
Now add back the prawns and the zucchini noodles. Stir together for a minute or two, until well-heated and combined. The zucchini should soften slightly, but not too much.
Remove into a bowl and top with grated parmesan and chopped parsley.

# Chicken and chickpea broccoli noodle pasta

Ingredients:

- 5 tbsp extra virgin olive oil
- 1 chicken breast (boneless)
- salt and pepper
- 1/4 tsp dried oregano flakes
- 1/2 cup canned chickpeas, drained and rinsed
- 2 broccoli stems
- 1/2 cup cooked green peas
- 1/2 cup thinly sliced leeks

For the dressing:

- 1/3 cup feta
- 1/2 shallot, chopped
- 1 small garlic clove, minced
- 2 tbsp basil, chopped
- salt and pepper
- 1 tbsp lemon juice
- 1 tbsp olive oil
- 1 tbsp red wine vinegar

## Directions

Place a large skillet over medium heat with olive oil in it. Meanwhile, season chicken with salt, pepper and oregano on both sides. When oil starts shimmering, add in the chicken and cook until no longer pink. Set aside.

Place a medium pot filled halfway with water over high heat and bring to a boil.

Using a Spiralizer, cut broccoli into noodles. When the water starts boiling, add in the broccoli noodles and peas, and then cook for 2-3 minutes. Drain and set aside.

While broccoli noodles are chilling, place all the ingredients for the feta dressing into a blender and pulse until creamy.

Take a large bowl; place the broccoli noodles, chickpeas, peas, leeks and dressing in and mix.

# Butternut Squash Noodles in Sage Brown Butter

Ingredients:

- 4 cups Spiralized butternut squash "noodles"
- 2 tsp extra virgin olive oil
- 4 tablespoons unsalted butter
- 10 medium fresh sage leaves
- salt and pepper
- grated parmesan cheese

Directions

Preheat oven to 400 degrees F.

Take a large baking sheet with parchment paper. Place the Spiralized squash noodles on the parchment and drizzle with the olive oil. Gently toss to coat with the oil. Bake for 7 minutes.

While noodles are cooking, melt the butter in a large skillet over medium heat, stirring constantly. Within 1-2 minutes, the butter will begin to brown; add the sage leaves at this time, stirring them until they are fragrant and darken. The entire process only takes 2-3 minutes. Remove from heat. Put the squash noodles in the browned butter to fully coat.

# Low-Carb Zucchini Pasta

## Ingredients:

- 3 zucchini
- anchovies
- handful of pitted black olives
- 2 cloves of garlic
- parmesan
- handful of capers
- chili flakes
- tin of tomatoes
- olive oil

## Directions

Get a pan nice and hot, and then turn down to medium heat.
Add a generous glug of olive oil, enough to coat the bottom. Crush
two cloves of garlic into the oil. Add three or four anchovies. The
anchovies should start to disintegrate in the oil and the garlic gently
brown and soften.
Add a sprinkle of chili flakes to the sizzling oil. Roughly chop up your
black olives and capers and add them, too. Give it all a good stir and
fry for 1 minute.
Add your tinned tomatoes. Let it all bubble away, stirring now and then
for a few minutes. Put to one side to cool.
Using a Spiralizer, cut your zucchini into ribbons; toss the sauce
through.
Add some fresh parmesan.

# Sweet Potato Curly Fries with Chipotle Lime Aioli

Ingredients:

- -2 large sweet potatoes
- -olive oil
- -salt and pepper
- -chipotle aioli

Directions

Preheat oven to 400 degrees F.

Spiralize sweet potatoes.

Take baking sheets with parchment paper. Add sweet potatoes and spread out evenly. Sprinkle with olive oil and season with salt and pepper. Bake potatoes for 35-40 minutes.

Meanwhile, for the aioli, combine Greek yogurt, lime juice and chipotle pepper in a blender.

Puree well and taste for seasoning and spiciness.

# Spiralized Latkes

Ingredients:

- 4 eggs
- 5 Yukon Gold potatoes, peeled
- 1/2 tsp black pepper
- 1 medium Spanish onion, peeled and very finely diced
- 2 tsp kosher salt
- 1/4 cup flour
- oil, for frying

Directions

Use a Spiralizer to get strings of potato spirals. Place in a large bowl.
Heat about 3/4 inch of oil over a medium flame.
Add the remaining ingredients to the bowl and stir to combine.
Once the oil is hot enough, spoon a small mound of the potato
mixture into the oil, makin sure the liquid doesn't get left behind. Stir
between every few latkes. Some of the potato strands might be long, so
break them up with your fingers. Fry for about 2 minutes, until golden,
then flip and fry for about another two minutes.

# Pumpkin Spice Sweet Potato Noodle Waffles

Ingredients:

- 1 medium sweet potato, peeled
- 1 medium egg, beaten
- 1 tsp pumpkin spice
- 1 tbsp maple syrup
- cooking spray

Directions

Heat up the waffle iron.
Place a large skillet over medium heat and coat with cooking spray.
Make noodles out of potatoes using a Spiralizer. Add the sweet potato
noodles to the skillet and cook, turning frequently, for about 10
minutes or until noodles have completely softened.
Add the noodles into a bowl and add in the pumpkin spice. Mix to
combine thoroughly.
Add in the full egg and toss to combine.
Coat the waffle iron with cooking spray and pack in the noodles. You
may have to play around with the noodles to get them to fit in all of the
grooves. Cook the waffle according to the iron's settings. Serve with
maple syrup.

## Ingredients:

- 1 tbsp extra virgin olive oil
- 1 cup frozen garden peas
- 1.5 pounds Yukon Gold potatoes, peeled
- salt and pepper, to taste

For the pesto:

- 2 tbsp pine nuts
- 2 packed cups of basil
- 2 tbsp parmesan cheese
- 3 tbsp extra virgin olive oil
- 1 large garlic clove
- salt and pepper, to taste

## Directions

Place a large skillet over medium-high heat with the olive oil in it. Use a Spiralizer to cut potatoes into noodles. When oil heats, add in the potato noodles and season with salt and pepper. Stir and then cover and cook, uncovering occasionally to stir, for 7-10 minutes or until potato noodles are cooked through. Place in a large mixing bowl. While the potatoes cook, add all of the ingredients for the pesto to a blender and pulse until creamy. Set aside. Cook your peas according to package directions.

Once potato noodles, peas and pesto are done, combine in a bowl and toss thoroughly.

Ingredients:

For the tofu:

- 1/4 cup low-sodium soy sauce
- 6.5 oz extra-firm tofu
- 1 tsp sesame oil

For the salad:

- 2 large carrots
- 3 cups watercress
- 1/2 tsp black sesame seeds + 1/2 tsp white sesame seeds, mixed

For the dressing:

- 2 tbsp extra virgin olive oil
- 2 tbsp rice vinegar
- 1 tsp white miso
- 1/2 tbsp sesame oil
- 1/2 inch piece of ginger, grated
- 1 tbsp of water
- salt and pepper, to taste

Directions

Preheat the oven to 350 degrees F. Take a baking sheet with parchment paper and set aside.

Press excess moisture out of the tofu by squeezing between two layers of paper towel. Repeat until moisture is absorbed.

Dice the tofu into cubes and place in a medium mixing bowl along with the other ingredients for the tofu. Let it marinate for 10 minutes and then arrange on the prepared baking tray.

While the tofu marinates, combine all the ingredients for the dressing and whisk together until combined.

Bake the tofu for 30 minutes or until browned and stiffened, flipping the tofu pieces over halfway through.

While tofu bakes, peel and Spiralize the carrots. Place the carrot noodles into a large mixing bowl and set aside. Ten minutes before the tofu is done cooking, drizzle the dressing over the carrot noodles and toss to combine. Place in the refrigerator until the tofu is done.

Once the tofu is done, add the watercress to the bowl with the carrots. Toss to combine and then plate the salad, top with tofu and garnish with sesame seed mix.

## Noodles Cacio e Pepe

Ingredients:

- 6 zucchinis
- 3/4 cup finely grated parmesan cheese
- 1/3 cup finely grated pecorino
- 1 tbsp ground black pepper
- 2 tbsp olive oil

Directions

Using a Spiralizer, create zucchini noodles. Heat one tablespoon of olive oil in a large pan over medium-high heat. Add zucchini noodles and cook for about 2-3 minutes, until zucchini noodles are tender but still retain some crunch.

Let the noodles rest for about 3 minutes so they can release all of the moisture. Remove noodles to a bowl and reserve the excess water in a small bowl. In another large bowl, combine the cheeses and black pepper; add just enough noodle water to make a thick paste.

Add noodles, and stir vigorously to coat them with the cheese-pepper sauce, adding some olive oil and a bit of noodle water to thin the sauce if necessary.

The sauce should cling to the noodles and be creamy but not watery.

If the noodles are not hot enough, heat them in the pan for a couple of minutes before serving.

Sprinkle with additional grated parmesan and pecorino cheese and pepper.

# Zucchini Noodles and Summer Vegetables with Sweet Pepper Chicken Sausage

Ingredients:

- 1/4 cup shredded parmesan cheese
- 2 zucchini
- 2 tbsp extra-virgin olive oil, divided
- 1 cup lightly torn fresh spinach
- 1/3 cup chopped white onion
- 1/2 cup chopped green bell pepper
- 1 tbsp seasoned salt
- 1 pinch sea salt and freshly ground black pepper to taste
- 1 tsp garlic paste
- 2 sweet pepper chicken sausages, sliced
- 2 tablespoons chopped fresh basil
- 1 large tomato, diced

Directions

Bring a pot of lightly salted water to a boil. Using a Spiralizer, cut zucchini into noodles. Cook noodles in the boiling water for about 3 minutes, then drain.

Heat 1 tablespoon olive oil in a skillet over medium heat; cook and stir green bell pepper, onion, seasoned salt, and sea salt for 3 minutes.

Add chicken sausage and cook until sausage is lightly browned, about 5 minutes. Add basil, spinach, garlic paste, and seasoned salt to taste; cook for 2-3 minutes.

Place noodles on a serving plate and toss with remaining tablespoon olive oil (1) and sea salt.

Add sausage mixture and tomatoes, and then top with Parmesan cheese; season with salt and pepper.

# Zoodles ala Carbonara

## Ingredients:
- 2 eggs
- 1 extra large zucchini
- 1 egg yolk
- 2 tbsp grated parmigiano-reggiano cheese
- 2/3 cup shredded pecorino cheese
- 2 tsp ground black pepper
- 2 tbsp olive oil
- 2 ounces cubed pancetta

## Directions

Whisk eggs and egg yolk together in a bowl. Add pecorino cheese and mix well.

Use a Spiralizer to cut zucchini into noodles. Heat olive oil in a large wok or skillet over medium heat; cook and stir pancetta for 2-3 minutes.

Add the noodles; cook and stir for about 3-5 minutes. Remove wok from heat.

Pour egg mixture over noodles and stir until evenly coated.

Top noodles with parmigiano-reggiano cheese and black pepper.

Ingredients:

- 3 zucchini
- 1 pound ground turkey
- 1/2 tsp garlic salt
- 1 tbsp salt
- 1/2 tsp onion powder
- 1/2 tsp garlic powder
- 1/4 tsp cayenne pepper
- 1 tsp minced garlic
- 1/4 tsp red pepper flakes
- 1 tsp olive oil
- 1 (14.5 ounce) can diced tomatoes
- 2 tsp dried parsley
- 1 (3 ounce) can tomato paste
- 2 tbsp balsamic vinegar
- 1 cup small-curd cottage cheese
- 1 cup shredded mozzarella cheese
- 1 tsp dried basil
- 1/2 tsp Italian seasoning
- 1/4 tsp ground black pepper
- 1/2 tsp salt

Directions

Make zucchini noodles using a Spiralizer.
Place noodles in a colander and cover liberally with 1 tablespoon salt.
Let it sit about 20 minutes. Rinse noodles and pat dry.
Place ground turkey, garlic salt and powder, onion powder, cayenne pepper, and red pepper flakes in a large oven-safe skillet over medium heat. Cook and stir about 5 minutes. Drain grease.

Push turkey to the sides of the skillet to make an empty space in the center.

Add olive oil and minced garlic; cook until garlic is fragrant (for 1 minute).

Preheat oven to 400 degrees F. Mix and place diced tomatoes, tomato paste, basil, Italian seasoning, balsamic vinegar, parsley, 1/2 teaspoon salt, and black pepper into the skillet. Bring to a boil; cook about 15 minutes.

Add in noodles. Cover with cottage cheese. Sprinkle mozzarella cheese evenly on top. Bake in the preheated oven until cheese is melted.

Turn on broiler and broil until cheese is golden brown.

Remove from oven and let sit for 5-10 minutes before serving.

## Ingredients:

Marinara Sauce:

- 2 ripe tomatoes, chopped
- 1/2 (8 ounce) can tomato paste
- 2 tbsp simple syrup
- 1 tbsp olive oil
- 2 tbsp chopped garlic
- 1/2 cup water, or as needed
- 2 tbsp balsamic vinegar
- 1 tsp sea salt

Spaghetti:

- 4 zucchini

## Directions

Add tomatoes, tomato paste, water, simple syrup, garlic, balsamic vinegar, olive oil, and sea salt to blender and blend on high-speed until smooth. Add more water if sauce is too thick.

Place Spiralized zucchini in a bowl; add sauce and mix.

## Ingredients:

- cooking spray (nonfat)
- 2 tbsp extra-virgin olive oil
- 1 1/2 tbsp seafood seasoning
- 1/2 tsp hot sauce
- 1 tbsp malt vinegar
- 1/2 tsp garlic powder
- 2 large russet potatoes
- sea salt to taste
- 1 tsp onion powder

## Directions

Preheat oven to 425 degrees F. Prepare 2 baking sheets with aluminum foil; spray with cooking spray.

Mix oil, seafood seasoning, onion powder, hot sauce, and garlic powder together in a bowl.

Cut potatoes using a Spiralizer; snip long spirals into smaller lengths. Place potatoes into a large bowl; drizzle with oil mixture. Mix until potatoes are coated.

Spread coated potatoes in a single layer onto the baking sheets, leaving 1/4-inch of space between potato spirals.

Bake in the preheated oven until bottom of potatoes are browned, it takes about 8-9 minutes. Flip potatoes.

Bake until potatoes are browned and crisp on top.

Sprinkle malt vinegar and sea salt over potatoes.

# Mexican Squash Noodles with Creamy Fire-Roasted Green Chile Sauce

## Ingredients:

- 1/4 cup milk
- 1 tbsp olive oil
- 3 cloves garlic, crushed
- 1/2 onion, cut into noodle shapes
- 1 (4 ounce) can fire-roasted diced green chili peppers
- 4 Mexican squash
- 1 (11 ounce) can Mexican-style corn, drained
- 4 ounces Neufchatel cheese, softened

## Directions

Using a Spiralizer, cut the Mexican squash. Heat oil in a skillet over medium flame. Add onion and garlic; cook and stir about 5 minutes. Add in squash and corn; cook, stirring frequently, about 5 minutes. Remove to individual serving plates.

Add Neufchatel cheese, chili peppers and milk in a blender; blend until sauce is smooth.

Heat sauce in a saucepan over medium heat about 2-4 minutes; pour over squash mixture.

# Spiralized Roasted Vanilla Sweet Potatoes and Apples

Ingredients:

- 1/4 cup olive oil
- cooking spray
- 1 large sweet potato, peeled and halved
- 1/3 vanilla bean
- 1 large Red Delicious apple, unpeeled
- 2 tbsp brown sugar
- 1/4 tsp salt
- 1/2 tsp ground cinnamon
- 1 pinch ground nutmeg ground ginger

Directions

Preheat oven to 400 degrees F. Prepare a baking sheet with aluminum foil; spray with cooking spray.

Split vanilla bean lengthwise with the tip of a sharp knife. Hold the pod open; scrape seeds from each half using the flat side of your knife.

Combine vanilla bean, scraped seeds, and olive oil in a small saucepan over very low heat. Warm the oil about 5 minutes. Remove from heat and let cool.

Using a Spiralizer cut sweet potato and apple into noodles. Place in a large bowl.

Whisk 2 tablespoons olive oil, brown sugar, salt, cinnamon, nutmeg, and ginger together in a small bowl.

Drizzle over sweet potato and apple; mix well to coat. Spread sweet potato and apple in an even layer on the prepared baking sheet. Bake in the preheated oven, turning once about 10 minutes. Increase oven temperature to 425 degrees F. Roast for 8 minutes more.

## Shrimp Florentine with Noodles

Ingredients:

- 1 tbsp butter
- 1 tbsp extra-virgin olive oil
- 2 zucchini
- 1/2 large yellow onion, minced
- 1 tbsp chopped garlic
- 1/2 tsp kosher salt
- 2 tbsp butter
- 1 pound large shrimp, peeled and deveined
- 1 tsp minced garlic
- 1 (6 ounce) bag baby spinach
- 1 tbsp fresh lemon juice
- 1 tsp red pepper flakes
- 1/2 tsp kosher salt
- 1/2 tsp freshly ground black pepper

Directions

Cut zucchini into noodles using a Spiralizer.
In a large skillet, heat 1 tablespoon butter and olive oil together over medium heat; add in zucchini noodles, onion, chopped garlic, and 1/2 teaspoon salt; cook and stir for 5 minutes.
Remove noodle mixture to a bowl.
Heat 2 tablespoons butter in the same skillet. Add in shrimp and minced garlic; cook and stir for 3-4 minutes. Add spinach, lemon juice, red pepper flakes, 1/2 teaspoon salt, and pepper; cook and stir until spinach begins to wilt (3-4 minutes).
Add noodle mixture; cook and stir until heated through (2-3 minutes).

# Grilled Shrimp over Zucchini Noodles

## Ingredients:
- 1 pound shrimp, peeled and deveined
- 5 zucchini
- 2 cups thinly sliced fresh basil
- 1/3 cup toasted sliced almonds, divided
- 1 tablespoon red wine vinegar
- 1 lemon, zested
- 1 shallot, coarsely chopped
- 9 tablespoons olive oil, divided
- 2 cloves garlic, coarsely chopped
- 1/4 teaspoon red pepper flakes
- kosher salt and freshly ground black pepper to taste

## Directions

Add basil, 1/2 cup olive oil, 1/4 cup almonds, vinegar, shallot, garlic, lemon zest, and red pepper flakes to blender and blend until smooth. In a skillet, heat 1 tablespoon olive oil over medium-high heat; sauté shrimp until cooked through and pink (2-4 minutes). Remove skillet from heat and mix shrimp with 2 tablespoons dressing in a bowl. Cut zucchini with a Spiralizer to create noodles. Add to skillet; cook and stir over medium heat until zucchini noodles are tender (1-2 minutes). Add 2 tablespoons lemon basil dressing and toss to coat. Remove skillet from heat. Arrange shrimp on top of zucchini noodles; season with salt and black pepper.
Top with remaining almonds.

# Shrimp Scampi Zucchini

Ingredients:

- 4 zucchini
- 3/4 cup butter, divided olive oil
- 1/4 cup grated parmesan cheese
- 1/4 cup diced onion
- 1 (15 ounce) can diced tomatoes
- 2 tablespoons crushed garlic
- 2 cups white wine
- 2 pounds uncooked medium shrimp, peeled and deveined
- 3 tbsp seafood seasoning
- 1/2 lemon, juiced
- salt and ground black pepper, to taste

Directions

In a large pot, melt 1/4 cup butter with olive oil over medium-high heat. Sauté onion and garlic in hot butter mixture until softened.
Add in shrimp, wine, diced tomatoes, and seafood seasoning with the onion mixture; cook and stir until shrimp turns pink (about 5 minutes).
Add 1/2 cup butter and lemon juice to the shrimp mixture; cook until the butter melts completely (1-2 minutes).
Season the mixture with salt and pepper. Cut zucchini using a Spiralizer. Add the zucchini and cook until tender, about 5 minutes more.
Top with parmesan cheese.

# Zucchini Noodles Pad Thai

## Ingredients:

- 3 large zucchini
- 1/4 cup chicken stock
- 12 ounces skinless, boneless chicken breasts cut into 1-inch cubes
- 2 1/2 tbsp tamarind paste
- 1 1/2 tbsp Asian chili pepper sauce
- 2 tbsp low-sodium soy sauce
- 1 tbsp Worcestershire sauce
- 2 tbsp oyster sauce
- 1 tbsp fresh lime juice
- 2 tbsp sesame oil
- 1 tbsp white sugar
- 1 tbsp chopped garlic
- 8 ounces peeled and deveined shrimp
- 2 eggs, beaten
- 2 tbsp water, or as needed (optional)
- 3 cups bean sprouts, divided
- 2 tbsp chopped unsalted dry-roasted peanuts
- 6 green onions, chopped into 1-inch pieces
- 1/4 cup chopped fresh basil

## Directions

Cut zucchini into noodles using a Spiralizer.
Whisk chicken stock, tamarind paste, soy sauce, oyster sauce, chili pepper sauce, Worcestershire sauce, lime juice, and sugar together in a small bowl to make a smooth sauce.

In a large skillet, heat sesame oil over high heat. Add garlic and stir for 10 seconds. Add chicken and shrimp; cook and stir until chicken is no longer pink in the center and the juices run clear (5-7 minutes).

Push chicken and shrimp to the sides of the skillet to make a space in the center. Pour eggs and scramble until firm, 2-3 minutes.

Add in zucchini noodles and sauce; cook and stir, adding water if needed, about 3 minutes.

Add 2 cups bean sprouts and green onions; cook and stir for 2 minutes. Remove skillet from heat and sprinkle peanuts over noodles. Serve garnished with remaining 1 cup bean sprouts and fresh basil.

# Deep-Fried Zucchini Spirals

Ingredients:

- 1 zucchini
- 1 egg
- 1 tbsp milk
- 1/4 cup cornstarch
- 1/2 cup all-purpose flour
- 3 cups vegetable oil
- 1 tsp seafood seasoning

Directions

Heat oil in a large saucepan to 350 degrees F.
Mix egg and milk together in a bowl; pour into a gallon-size resealable plastic bag.
Combine flour and cornstarch together in another bowl; pour into a separate gallon-size resealable plastic bag.
Cut zucchinis into noodles with a Spiralizer. Place noodles into milk mixture, seal the bag, and turn to coat spirals completely. Transfer zucchini to flour mixture, seal the bag, and shake gently to coat completely. Remove noodles from flour mixture and shake gently to remove any excess flour.
Working in batches, cook zucchini noodles in the preheated oil until golden brown and cooked through (2-4 minutes). Remove zucchini to a paper towel-lined plate to drain. Sprinkle seafood seasoning over cooked zucchini noodles.

# Lemon Herb Chicken with Zucchini Pasta and Ricotta

Ingredients:

- 4 skinless, boneless chicken breast halves, cut into strips
- 4 cloves garlic
- 4 zucchini squash
- minced lemon, zested
- 1 1/2 cups ricotta cheese
- 1 tbsp chopped fresh chives
- 1 tsp fresh oregano
- 1 tsp fresh thyme
- 1/4 cup olive oil, plus more for pan
- 1/2 tsp salt
- 1/4 tsp ground black pepper
- 2 fresh tomatoes, diced
- 1 pinch red pepper flakes salt and ground black pepper to taste
- chopped lemon, juiced
- 4 fresh basil leaves

Directions

Place chicken, garlic, lemon zest, chives, thyme, oregano, 1/2 teaspoon salt, 1/4 teaspoon pepper, and 1/4 cup olive oil in a resealable plastic bag; toss to coat chicken and refrigerate for 3 hours or up to overnight. Heat a large skillet over medium heat; cook and stir chicken with marinade until chicken is no longer pink at the center and juices run clear, about 8 minutes.

Remove chicken from pan; set aside to keep warm. Cut zucchini into noodles with a Spiralizer.

Add about 1 teaspoon oil into the same skillet over medium-high heat; stir in zucchini and red pepper flakes and cook about 3 minutes; season with salt and pepper.

Add ricotta cheese and basil into zucchini; cook until heated through, about 2 minutes. Return chicken to pan with zucchini mixture; stir to combine.

Remove pan from heat, squeeze lemon juice over entire dish, and garnish with diced tomatoes.

## Ingredients:

- 1 pound ground beef
- 1 tsp ground black pepper
- 1 (15 ounce) can tomato sauce
- 1 (14.5 ounce) can whole peeled tomatoes
- 1 tbsp salt, or more to taste
- 1 tsp dried basil
- 1/2 tsp dried oregano
- 1/2 tsp garlic powder
- 1/2 tsp onion powder
- 1/4 tsp ground thyme
- 1/4 tsp red pepper flakes
- 1 (6 ounce) can tomato paste
- 3 zucchini

## Directions

Heat a large skillet over medium-high heat.

Cook and stir beef and black pepper in the hot skillet until browned and crumbly, 5 to 7 minutes; drain and discard grease.

Add in tomato sauce, tomatoes, salt, basil, oregano, garlic powder, onion powder, thyme, and red pepper flakes to ground beef; cook and stir until sauce is warmed through, about 2 minutes.

Stir tomato paste into sauce.

Cut zucchini into noodles with a Spiralizer.

Add noodles into sauce, pressing down to fully submerge them; simmer over medium-low heat until zucchini is tender, about 10 minutes.

# Zucchini Pasta with Roasted Red Pepper Sauce and Chicken

Ingredients:

- 6 Roma tomatoes
- 2 yellow summer squash
- 3 red bell peppers, chopped
- 1 (28 ounce) can crushed tomatoes
- 1 large sweet onion, halved
- 2 zucchini
- 3 tbsp extra-virgin olive oil
- 1 cup tightly packed fresh basil leaves, chopped salt and ground black pepper to taste
- 4 cloves garlic
- 2 cooked chicken breast halves, cubed
- 1 tbsp grated parmesan cheese, or to taste

Directions

Preheat grill for medium heat and lightly oil the grate.
Grill tomatoes, bell peppers, and onion halves on the preheated grill about 15 minutes.
When peppers are cool enough to handle, split with a knife and remove seeds. Heat olive oil in a large skillet, add garlic, cook and stir until fragrant.
Add canned crushed tomatoes, bell peppers, basil, grilled tomatoes, and onion into skillet; bring to a boil, reduce heat, and simmer until vegetables are tender, about 10 minutes.
Puree vegetable mixture with a stick blender; season with salt and pepper and keep at a simmer.
Bring a large pot of water to a boil.
While boiling, cut zucchini and summer squash into noodles with a Spiralizer.

Once boiled, drop in all the noodles and cook until tender, about 3 minutes. Drain water from pot; lay noodles on paper towels to drain completely.

Place noodles on individual plates; top with a portion of cooked chicken, a generous amount of red pepper sauce, and parmesan cheese.

# Apple-Potato Latkes

Ingredients:
- 1 firm apple, peeled
- 1 russet potato, peeled
- 1 egg, lightly beaten
- 1/2 tsp sea salt
- 3 tbsp all-purpose flour
- 2 tbsp vegetable oil, or as needed
- 1 tsp maple syrup
- 1/2 tsp sea salt
- 1 pinch ground nutmeg

Directions

Make a deep vertical cut on each side of the potato and apple.
Use a Spiralizer to cut potato into thin shreds. Repeat with apple.
Spread shredded potato and apple on several layers of paper towels;
squeeze to release as much moisture as possible. Remove to a bowl.
Add in egg, flour, maple syrup, salt, and nutmeg. Heat vegetable oil in a
skillet over medium heat.
Spoon 2 tablespoons of the potato mixture into the skillet; flatten
slightly with a spatula. Cook until golden brown on both sides. Drain
on a plate lined with paper towels.
Repeat with remaining mixture, adding more oil if needed.

## Ingredients:

- 2 zucchinis
- 1/2 cup pecorino Romano cheese, grated
- 2 tbsp olive oil
- pinch of oregano flakes
- salt and pepper
- 1/2 bunch broccoli rabe
- 2 cloves of garlic, minced
- 1 tsp red pepper flakes
- 1/2 cup chicken broth
- 1 tbsp juice from a lemon
- 2 spicy Italian sausage links (or chicken sausage)

## Directions

Prepare your broccoli rabe. Rinse the leaves and pat dry. Cut off most of the stems (the thickest parts). Pull off some skin of the stems, using a peeler. Peel until you hit the leaves. Set aside.

Place a large skillet over medium heat and add in the olive oil. Slice the sausage into 1/2 inch chunks and place into skillet along with the garlic and season with salt, pepper, and a pinch of oregano. Cook for about 3 minutes, flipping over to cook both sides.

Push the sausage to the side and add the broccoli rabe and red pepper flakes to the skillet. Stir and cook for about 1 minute and then add in the chicken broth, mixing the sausage and broccoli rabe together. Cook until reduced and broccoli rabe is mostly wilted. Cut zucchini into noodles with a Spiralizer. Then, add noodles to the skillet. Cook for about 2 minutes. Stir in pecorino Romano cheese and lemon juice and combine thoroughly.

# Desserts

# Apple Pie

Yield: Makes: 8 portions
Cooking Time: 45 minutes

## Ingredients

- 2 refrigerated pie crusts
- 2½ pound honey crisp apples, spiralized with Blade C
- 1 tablespoon fresh lemon juice
- 1 cup granulated sugar
- ¼ cup cornstarch
- ½ teaspoon ground cinnamon
- ½ teaspoon ground ginger
- 1 teaspoon vanilla extract
- 2 tablespoons unsalted butter, cut into 8 cubes
- Cream, as required
- Powdered sugar, as required

## Directions

Preheat the oven to 375 degrees F.

Unroll 1 prepared pie crust into a circle large enough to fit into a 9-inch pie dish. Arrange the crust in the pie dish, cutting and folding excess dough underneath the edges to create a scalloped crust edge. With a fork, prick the holes across the bottom of the crust. Freeze the pie dish for at least 15 minutes.

In a bowl, add apple noodles and lemon juice and toss to coat.

In another bowl, mix together sugar, cornstarch, cinnamon, and ginger. Add the sugar mixture into the bowl of apple noodles and toss to coat. Transfer the apple filling into the prepared crust. Place the butter cubes over the filling evenly. Unroll the second round of pie dough and cut into 1-inch-wide strips. Top the pie with the strips in a lattice pattern, making slits in the crust so that steam can escape. Brush the top crust with cream and sprinkle with the sugar.

Bake for about 45 minutes. Remove from oven and keep on a wire rack to cool completely.

Cut into desired slices and serve.

Yield: Makes: 8 portions
Cooking Time: 40 minutes

<u>Ingredients</u>

For Filling

- 2 (1-pound) sweet potatoes, peeled and spiralized with Blade C
- ¼ cup unsalted butter, melted
- ½ teaspoon ground cinnamon
- ¼ teaspoon ground nutmeg
- Salt, to taste
- ½ cup water

For Topping:
- 1/3 cup all-purpose flour
- ¼ cup brown sugar
- ½ cup pecans, chopped
- Salt, to taste
- ¼ cup unsalted butter, cubed
- 2 cups mini marshmallows

<u>Directions</u>
Preheat the oven to 375°F. Grease a 13x9-inch baking dish.
In a large bowl, add the sweet potato noodles, melted butter, spices and salt and gently toss to coat. Transfer the sweet potato mixture into the prepared baking dish. Place the water over the sweet potatoes. With a piece of foil, cover the baking dish and bake for about 20-25 minutes. Meanwhile for topping in a bowl, mix together flour, sugar, pecans and salt. Slowly, add the butter and mix until crumbly mixture forms.

Remove the baking dish from the oven and top with the pecan mixture and marshmallows evenly. Bake for about 15 minutes.
Serve warm.

Yield: Makes: 6 portions
Cooking Time: 10 minutes

<u>Ingredients</u>

- 4 medium tart apples, peeled, spiralized with Blade C and chopped
- 2/3 cup old-fashioned oats
- 2/3 cup brown sugar
- ½ cup Bisquick mix
- 3 tablespoons butter, softened
- ¾ teaspoon ground cinnamon
- ¾ teaspoon ground nutmeg

<u>Directions</u>
In the bottom of an ungreased 8-inch square microwave safe dish, arrange apple noodles.
In a small bowl, add remaining ingredients and mix until crumbly mixture forms. Spread the crumble mixture over apples evenly.
Microwave, uncovered on High for about 7-10 minutes, rotating dish after 5 minutes.
Serve warm.

# Pear Crumble

Yield: Makes: 8 portions
Cooking Time: 40 minutes

Ingredients

For Filling

- 9 medium pears, spiralized with Blade C
- 1/3 cup brown sugar
- 1 teaspoon ground cinnamon
- 3 tablespoons fresh orange juice
- 2 teaspoons fresh orange zest, grated finely

For Topping
- 1 cup rolled oats
- 1 cup almond meal
- 1/3 cup brown sugar
- 1 teaspoon ground cinnamon
- Pinch of ground nutmeg
- Pinch of salt
- ¼ cup coconut oil, melted

Directions
Preheat oven to 350 degrees F. Grease a 13x9-inch baking dish.
For filling in a large bowl, mix together pear noodles, sugar,
cinnamon, orange juice and zest.
In another bowl, mix together oats, almond meal, sugar,
cinnamon, nutmeg, and salt. Slowly, add coconut oil and mix until
crumbly mixture forms.
Transfer the pear mixture into the prepared baking dish evenly.
Top with crumb mixture evenly. Bake for about 40 minutes.

Serve warm.

# Zucchini Cookies

Yield: Makes: 12 portions
Cooking Time: 12 minutes

## Ingredients

- 1 cup flour
- 1 teaspoon baking soda
- ¾ teaspoon ground cinnamon
- Salt, to taste
- ¾ cup brown sugar
- ¼ cup apple butter
- 1 large egg
- 1 teaspoon vanilla extract
- 1 cup zucchini, spiralized with Blade C and chopped
- 2 cups rolled oats
- ½ cup white mini chocolate chips

## Directions

Preheat the oven to 350 degrees F. Line a cookie sheet with a parchment paper.

In a bowl, mix together flour, baking soda, cinnamon, and salt.

In another large bowl, add brown sugar and apple butter and beat until smooth. Add egg and vanilla and beat till well combined. Add flour mixture to egg mixture and mix until just combined. Fold in the zucchini, oats and chocolate chips.

With 1 tablespoon, place the mixture onto prepared cookie sheet about 3-inch apart. Bake for about 11-12 minutes or till the edges become golden brown.

Remove from the oven and keep onto the wire rack to cool in the pan for about 5 minutes. Carefully, invert the cookies onto the wire rack to cool completely.

## Ingredients:

For the filling:

- 10 Granny Smith apples, peeled with ends cut flat
- 1 teaspoon ground cinnamon
- 2 tablespoons fresh lemon juice
- 1/4 cup brown sugar
- 3/4 cup granulated sugar
- 1 tablespoon all-purpose flour

For the crisp:

- 1 teaspoon ground cinnamon
- 1 cup all-purpose flour
- 1 1/4 cup old fashioned oats
- 1/2 teaspoon nutmeg
- 1 cup brown sugar
- 1 teaspoon pure vanilla extract
- 1/2 cup butter, melted and cooled

## Directions:

Preheat oven to 350° F; butter a 9x13 inch baking dish. Cut apples into noodles with a Spiralizer.

Prepare the fruit base: In a large mixing bowl, combine and toss apple and lemon juice. In a medium bowl, mix granulated sugar, brown sugar, flour and cinnamon. Sprinkle sugar mixture over apples, tossing to coat. Pour apple mixture into prepared pan, spread into an even layer. Next, prepare the topping: In a large bowl, combine the oats, flour, cinnamon, nutmeg and brown sugar. Mix butter and vanilla together and pour over oat mixture; stir to combine. Crumble mixture evenly over the apples. Bake in preheated oven for 40-45 minutes. Serve warm. If desired, top with vanilla ice cream, caramel sauce, or whipped cream.

# Spiralized Apple "Spaghetti" with Cinnamon Dressing

Ingredients:
- 1 Red Delicious apple
- 2 tsp honey, or more to taste
- 1 (6 ounce) container plain Greek yogurt
- 1/4 tsp ground cinnamon
- 1/4 cup chopped walnuts
- 1/4 tsp vanilla extract

Directions:
Use a Spiralizer to cut an apple into ribbons. Add and mix Greek yogurt, honey, cinnamon, and vanilla extract together in a bowl. Add apple; toss to coat. Garnish with walnuts.

## Spiralized Carrot Cinnamon Pudding

Ingredients:

- 2 cups Spiralized carrots
- 2 tbsp + 1/4 tsp coconut oil
- 2 tbsp honey
- 2 tsp + 1 tsp cinnamon

Directions:

Place Spiralized carrots in a skillet with 1/4 teaspoon coconut oil. Sauté for 5 minutes.

Put remaining coconut oil, honey, and 2 teaspoons cinnamon in a pot. Place on low heat and stir consistently for maximum 5 minutes. Avoid burning or overcooking by keeping heat low and stirring continuously. Remove sauce from stove and add to the carrots. Return carrot mixture back to stove and turn on medium heat for 15 minutes. Serve warm.

# Chocolate-Coated Apple Drizzle

Ingredients:

- 2-3 apples
- 4 tbsp cacao
- 3 tbsp solid coconut oil
- 3 tbsp maple syrup
- 2 tablespoons sliced almonds

Directions:

Mix coconut oil and cacao in a pot. Place pot on stove and stir (continuously) on low heat for 4-5 minutes. Remove from heat and add in maple syrup. If desired, allow to sit for 20-30 minutes to thicken. It takes an hour for the chocolate to completely solidify, so make sure to use as sauce in under an hour. Use a Spiralizer to cut apples into noodles. Place 1 apple in each serving dish.

Garnish apples with sliced almonds or other topping of choice. Top off apples and almonds with melted chocolate sauce.

# Conclusion

There are a lot of healthy recipes when you use a Spiralizer, but it is important to experiment. Think about your own recipe and create new incredible dishes!

# About the Author

JULIA NELSON is an experienced chef, a food blogger, freelance recipe developer, writer, and cookbooks author.
Julia is passionate about fun, simple, healthy cooking such as slow cooker, instant pot, crock pot, electric pressure cooker recipes, baking recipes, spiralizer recipes, the list goes on.
Julia lives in California with her husband and three children. While not cooking, inventing new recipes and writing new books, Julia loves practicing jogging, photographing and exploring local farmer's market.

Find other Julia's books on her page on Amazon
www.amazon.com/author/julianelson

# Your Free Gift

I wanted to show my appreciation that you support my work so I've put together a free gift for you.

## LINK TO YOUR FREE GIFT

Just visit the link above to download it now.

I know you will love this gift.

Thanks!

Julia Nelson

Made in the USA
Lexington, KY
08 March 2019